Note Taking

Lessons to Improve Research Skills and Test Scores

BY
DEBORAH WHITE BROADWATER

COPYRIGHT © 2003 Mark Twain Media, Inc.

ISBN 10-digit: 1-58037-253-8
       13-digit: 978-1-58037-253-4

Printing No. CD-1597

Mark Twain Media, Inc., Publishers
Distributed by Carson-Dellosa Publishing Company, Inc.

TABLE OF CONTENTS

INTRODUCTION TO THE TEACHER

Note taking is an important skill for students to learn and understand. Being able to read an article or book and decide what is the important information will enable students to study for tests and do research. It is also important to understand that note taking will help a student to remember what has been said in class or written in the book after the lecture is over or the book has been closed.

This book is intended to offer the teacher and the parent lessons in helping the student to practice note taking. In this book, there are explanations about how to take notes from text-books, novels, for research, from online sources, and from lectures. There are also pages for practice. At the end of the book, there is a resource section for further explanation of some of the techniques. It may be helpful to give each student a copy of the resource section to keep in their notebooks or binders.

Teachers and parents may use these activities when teaching note taking to a whole class, to small groups, or to the individual student.

INTRODUCTION TO THE STUDENT

It is difficult to remember what you read or hear if you only read or hear it once. The best way to remember information is to hear or read it and then write it down. If you just listen to the teacher talk or just read a chapter once, you will be more likely to forget what was said or read when you hear and read other information, such as another class lesson or plans with your friends after school. Some information will be forgotten as soon as you walk out of the classroom, and most will be forgotten in a few days or a few weeks.

Taking notes helps you to better understand what was said by the teacher or written in your textbook. When you take good notes, you are listening or reading carefully with a purpose. You have to organize what the teacher says or what you read. You question what the teacher says or what you read, and you should be constantly thinking about the lecture or the book. Notes can be taken as lists, as summaries, or as whatever helps you remember. The more often you take notes in class and practice, the better you will be able to do it. The important thing is for you to find a style that is good for you.

NOTE TAKING FROM TEXTBOOKS

Taking notes from books is important. As you read your history or science or other textbook, you need to take notes to help you remember.

You need to take notes in an organized way. One way to organize your notes is to have a spiral-type notebook for each class. With a spiral, all the pages will be kept together. Another way is to use a three-ring binder. You will need to divide it into sections for each class.

Begin each note-taking session with a new sheet of paper. Make sure you write the date at the top. This is important to know so that when you go back to refer to the notes, you will know where to look.

Look over the section of text you will be reading. Notice the chapter title; ask yourself what the chapter is about. Then read the headings. These will give you clues as to what is important in the chapter. Make sure you notice the boldface words, the pictures, maps, diagrams, and charts. Look at the bottom of the pages to see if there are any footnotes or vocabulary definitions. All of these things will give you clues as to what will be important in the reading.

Next, write the chapter or section title in your notes. Then read the selection carefully. As you come to main ideas, write them in your notes. Write down subheadings and details that go with the subheadings. For example, if you are reading about France, and the subheading is farming, write down words or phrases that tell about farming in France. Write down boldface words and their meanings. Write down new vocabulary words and their meanings. Make sure that you include dates and what happened on those dates. Always write your notes in your own words. Summarize information, use a web, or use a chart or list to help you remember. Make sure that if you include information directly from the text, you put the information in quotation marks. You don't need to put a whole chart in your notes, you can just summarize the information.

Write clearly. Make sure that when you go back to read and study your notes for a test or a class discussion, you are able to read and understand what you wrote.

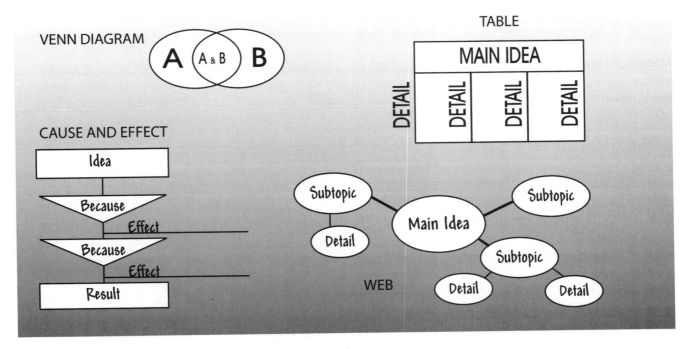

Name: _____   Date: _____

NOTE TAKING FROM TEXTBOOKS: PRACTICE 1

Exercise: Read the following paragraph, and fill in the information requested below.

Abraham Lincoln

Early Life

Abraham Lincoln was born on February 12, 1809, in Kentucky. He was the second child of Thomas and Nancy Lincoln. Abe Lincoln had an older sister named Sarah. The Lincoln family moved to Indiana in 1816, where Abe's mother died. His father then married a woman who had three children. One of Lincoln's jobs was to make fence poles from logs; this is how he got the nickname of "rail-splitter." Abe Lincoln didn't have much formal education. He could write and do simple arithmetic, and he loved to read. In 1830, his family moved to Illinois.

Topic: _____

Heading: _____

Important dates: _____

Important names: _____

Vocabulary words: _____

Important fact: _____

Important fact: _____

Important fact: _____

Important fact: _____

Name: _____ Date: _____

NOTE TAKING FROM TEXTBOOKS: PRACTICE 2

Exercise: Read the following paragraph, and take notes below.

Fuel

Solid Fuels

Coal, wood, charcoal, and peat are all solid fuels. Coal is made up of carbon and carbon compounds. It produces the most heat of the solid fuels. There are three types of coal: anthracite, lignite, and bituminous. Each type of coal is used in different areas. Wood produces little heat in comparison to coal. It was widely used for heating and cooking in the early days of America. Now it is used mostly in underdeveloped areas of the world. Charcoal comes from wood and produces a little more heat. It gives off a gas, so it is often used for cooking food outside. Peat is a poor fuel and is very smoky. It is made of dry vegetation and was used in Great Britain.

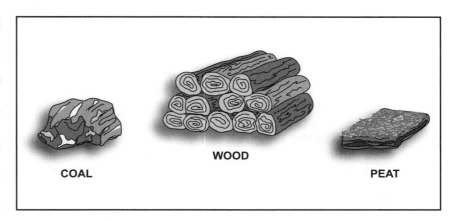

COAL   WOOD   PEAT

Topic: _____

Heading: _____

Vocabulary words: _____

Types of solid fuel: _____

Important detail: _____

Important detail: _____

Important detail: _____

Important detail: _____

Name: _____ Date: _____

Note Taking From Textbooks: Practice 3

Exercise: Read the following paragraph, and fill in the requested information below.

Alaska

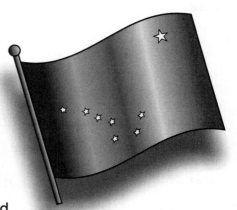

Alaska is the forty-ninth state in the United States. The territory was purchased in 1867 from Russia. Secretary of State William Seward got Congress to approve the purchase. Because of the distance to Alaska and the climate of the area, it was referred to as "Seward's Folly" or "Seward's Icebox." At first salmon fishing was the main industry, but gold was discovered in 1880. This started the Alaskan Gold Rush. Alaska now has a thriving oil business. A pipeline stretches across most of the state. It has brought money to the people from the taxes the petroleum industry pays. Alaska is the largest state in the union. Over 100 million acres of land have been set aside as national parks. Do you think it was Seward's Folly?

Topic: _____

Dates: _____

Vocabulary words: _____

Important detail: _____

Important detail: _____

Important detail: _____

Important detail: _____

Important detail: _____

Name: _____ Date: _____

NOTE TAKING FROM TEXTBOOKS: PRACTICE 4

Exercise: Read the following selection, and fill in the requested information below.

Aluminum

What lightweight metal makes up seven percent of the earth's crust? If you said aluminum, you would be correct. Pure aluminum is soft, but when made into an alloy with another metal, it becomes strong and hard. Aluminum conducts both heat and electricity.

Uses

New uses for aluminum and aluminum alloy are being found all the time. Because of its strength and durability, it is used in construction. Doors, shutters, and siding on houses are made of aluminum. This helps with the cost of building. In transportation, it is used on cars and boats. This is because it is lightweight and doesn't rust. Aluminum is used in industry to give paint a metallic finish. It also helps when metal roofs are painted to reflect the sun and its heat. Aluminum has other uses in cans and patio furniture, in space travel, and as aluminum foil, which is used to cook and store food.

Topic: _____

Heading: _____

Vocabulary words: _____

Important detail: _____

Important detail: _____

Important detail: _____

Important detail: _____

Important detail: _____

Cars

Baseball Bats

Boats

Siding

Name: _____ Date: _____

NOTE TAKING FROM TEXTBOOKS: CHRONOLOGICAL ORDER 1

Exercise: Read the following paragraphs. Take notes and put them in chronological order on the lines below.

The Civil War began on April 12, 1861, with shots fired at Fort Sumter, South Carolina. This was a victory for the Confederate army. The Battle of Bull Run occurred on July 21, 1861, at Manassas, Virginia. During this battle, the war was within 25 miles of Washington, D.C. An  important battle at sea was between the *Merrimack* and the *Monitor.* This battle took place March 8, 1862. These ships were called ironclads. For three days, the Confederate and Union armies fought at Gettysburg, Pennsylvania. This battle began on July 1, 1863, and ended July 3, 1863. Almost 50,000 men died at Gettysburg. On April 9, 1865, General Robert E. Lee signed the surrender of the Confederate army at Appomattox Courthouse, Virginia. This brought an end to the last war fought in the United States.

_____

_____

_____

_____

_____

_____

_____

_____

_____

Name: _____   Date: _____

NOTE TAKING FROM TEXTBOOKS: CHRONOLOGICAL ORDER 2

Exercise: Read the following paragraphs. Take notes and put them in chronological order on the lines below.

James Garfield

James A. Garfield was the twentieth president of the United States. He served from March 4, 1881, to his death on September 19, 1881. On July 2, 1881, he was shot by an assassin while at a train station.

Garfield was born November 19, 1831, in Orange, Ohio. He served as a congressman from Ohio from December 1863 to December 1879. In January 1880, he was elected as one of Ohio's senators.

James Garfield was married in 1858 to Lucretia Randolph. They had five boys and two girls.

Garfield was buried in Cleveland, Ohio.

_____

_____

_____

_____

_____

_____

_____

_____

_____

Name: _____ Date: _____

NOTE TAKING FROM TEXTBOOKS: SUMMARY 1

Exercise: Read the following paragraph, and then on the lines below, write a summary.

Have you ever wanted to look out into outer space and see the stars and planets as more than little specks in the sky? Then you need a telescope. A telescope helps objects appear closer. There are two types of telescopes, a refracting telescope and a reflecting telescope. The first telescopes were refracting telescopes. A refracting telescope bends or refracts light. The reflecting telescope reflects light. Sir Isaac Newton invented the reflecting telescope. Telescopes come in many sizes from the small to use at home or in your yard to the enormous that would be found at an observatory.

_____

_____

_____

_____

_____

Name: _____ Date: _____

NOTE TAKING FROM TEXTBOOKS: SUMMARY 2

Exercise: Read the following selection, and write a summary on the lines provided.

When it rains or snows, most of the water evaporates. The precipitation that doesn't evaporate is called runoff. One of the ways that runoff occurs is when there is a heavy downpour and the ground cannot absorb all of the rain. If the area has steep hills or has many streets and sidewalks made of concrete, there is a lot of runoff. If the soil is made of clay, the water will not absorb quickly, and the rain will run off. Often during times of several days of rainfall, the ground becomes overly saturated with water, and the new rain does not soak into the ground. This will also cause runoff. All of this water makes its way back to the ocean.

_____

_____

_____

_____

_____

Name: _____   Date: _____

NOTE TAKING FROM TEXTBOOKS: OUTLINE 1

Exercise: Organize these notes about England under the correct outline heading. Place the Roman numeral for the correct heading on the line next to each fact.

I.   Climate

II. Industry

III. Farming

IV. Government

_____ 1. The annual temperature is about 50 degrees Fahrenheit.

_____ 2. England has a House of Lords and a House of Commons.

_____ 3. There is fog and mist in much of England.

_____ 4. Coal mining has declined.

_____ 5. Cattle and sheep are raised for meat.

_____ 6. It rains about 30 inches per year.

_____ 7. A prime minister governs England.

_____ 8. Pottery was made in Birmingham.

_____ 9. The queen has very little governmental authority.

_____ 10. England has small family farms.

Name: _____ Date: _____

NOTE TAKING FROM TEXTBOOKS: OUTLINE 2

Exercise: Organize these notes about Benjamin Franklin under the correct outline heading. Place the Roman numeral for the correct heading on the line next to each fact.

I. Childhood

II. Inventor

III. Statesman

_____ 1. Benjamin Franklin was one of seventeen children.

_____ 2. Member of the Continental Congress

_____ 3. Postmaster General of the Colonies

_____ 4. Developed bifocal glasses

_____ 5. Apprenticed with a printer

_____ 6. Developed directions for using a lightning rod

_____ 7. Ambassador to France

_____ 8. Was ten years old when he left school

_____ 9. Served on the committee to write the Declaration of Independence

_____ 10. Experimented with lightning and electricity

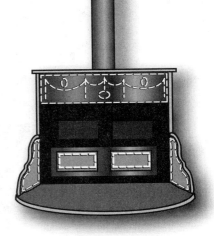

Name: _____   Date: _____

NOTE TAKING FROM TEXTBOOKS: TABLE

Exercise: Take notes from this selection, and use the table web.

That snake you see in your backyard is probably a garter snake. Garter snakes have yellow stripes, and some have dark squares like checks between the stripes. Garter snakes are usually between 18 and 30 inches long, but they have occasionally grown longer. They have thick bodies. Garter snakes eat frogs and tadpoles if they live near water. If they are not near water, they eat other small mammals or birds. Garter snakes don't lay eggs; they give birth to live young.

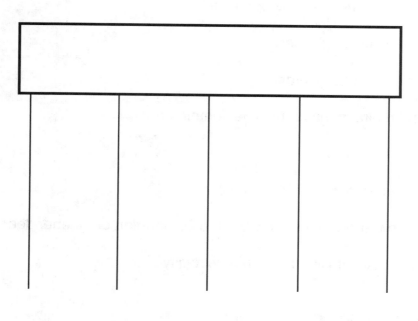

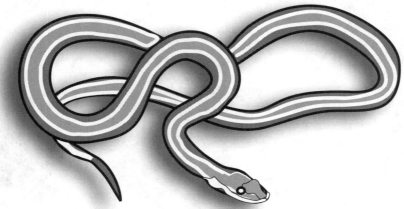

Name: _____   Date: _____

NOTE TAKING FROM TEXTBOOKS: CAUSE AND EFFECT

Exercise: Read the following paragraph. Take notes by filling in the cause-and-effect chart.

Some scientists believe that the temperature of the earth is increasing. This is called global warming. Scientists think that one thing causing this is the cutting down of the rain forests. Because of poverty in the jungles of South America, the natives clear the rain forests to plant crops and build homes. With less rain forests, there are fewer trees to produce oxygen, and this causes more greenhouse gases. Greenhouse gases are believed by some scientists to affect the ozone layer of the atmosphere. This would mean that more of the sun's rays will come directly to the earth rather than being filtered by the ozone layer, and the temperature will rise.

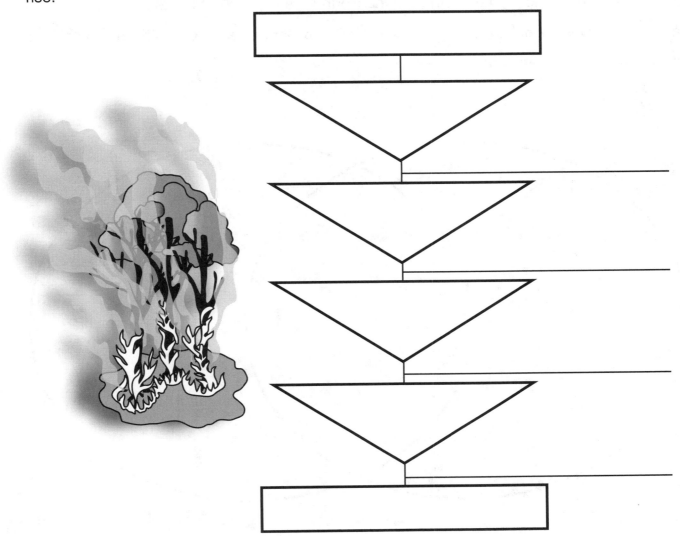

Name: _____ Date: _____

NOTE TAKING FROM TEXTBOOKS: VENN DIAGRAM 1

Exercise: Read the following paragraph. Take notes by filling in the Venn diagram.

Longitude and Latitude

If you look at a globe or a map, you will see lines drawn in a grid pattern. These lines help you locate positions around the globe. They are called latitude and longitude lines. Latitude lines go around the earth from east to west and measure distance north and south of the equator. Each one is parallel to the others, beginning at 0 degrees at the equator and continuing to 90 degrees at the pole. Lines of longitude are not parallel. They are farther apart at the equator and closer together at the poles. Longitude lines run north and south from the North Pole to the South Pole and measure distance east or west, beginning at 0 degrees at the Prime Meridian and continuing to 180 degrees at the International Date Line.

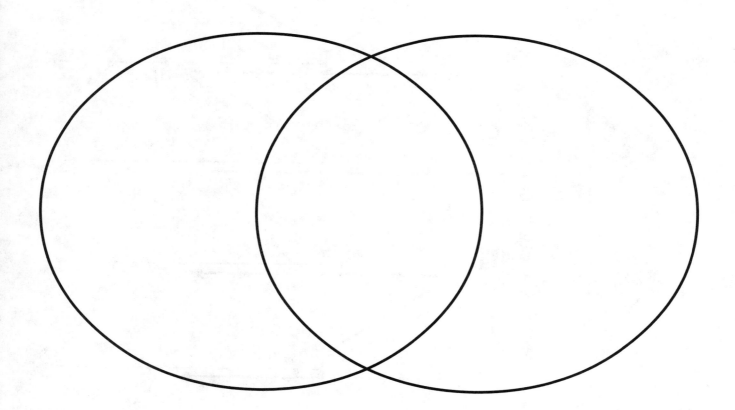

Name: _____ Date: _____

NOTE TAKING FROM TEXTBOOKS: VENN DIAGRAM 2

Exercise: Read the following story and fill in the Venn diagram comparing the two types of pets.

Pets

Choosing a pet can be a difficult decision. There are many unique pets, but most people choose between dogs and cats.

A cat is an independent animal that often does exactly what it chooses. It is hard to teach a cat tricks. There are many different breeds of cats—long and short hair and big and little. The colors vary depending on the breed. Cats are good pets if you don't have a lot of room because they can stay indoors. All they require is food and water and a litter box.

If you have room, a dog is a good choice for a pet. A dog needs to go outside and run in the yard or go for a walk. They are easier to teach tricks to and want lots of attention. There are also many breeds of dogs and many sizes.

Maybe it would be a good plan to have a cat and a dog.

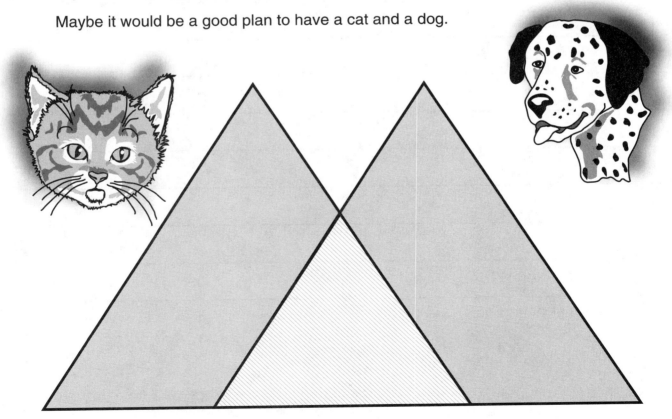

Name: _____ Date: _____

NOTE TAKING FROM TEXTBOOKS: LIST

Exercise: Read the following paragraph, and take notes in a list form.

To make chocolate chip cookies, you need to do several things. First, get out all of your ingredients. You will need brown and white sugar, butter, flour, baking soda, salt, vanilla, and eggs. You should then get out your utensils—a bowl, measuring spoons and cups, and a wooden spoon to stir. You also need at least one cookie sheet. Mix the butter and the sugars together; this is called creaming. Then add the eggs and vanilla and stir well. Add the flour, baking soda, and salt. When mixed well, stir in the chocolate chips. Drop spoonfuls of the dough on the cookie sheet so they are about three inches apart. Bake for 9–12 minutes in a 350-degree oven. Take the cookies off the sheet to cool and then eat.

_____

_____

_____

_____

_____

_____

_____

_____

_____

Name: _____ Date: _____

NOTE TAKING FROM TEXTBOOKS: WEB 1

Exercise: Read the following information and take notes using a web. Write the main idea in the center circle and the topic details in the other circles. Expand the web as needed.

Elements of Fiction

Plot

In fiction, the plot is all of the things that happen moment to moment in the story. Within the plot is the conflict, which is the problem in the story. There are two types of conflict, external and internal. The high point of the plot is the climax, and the resolution is when the conflict is resolved and the story comes to an end.

Setting

The setting is the time and place at which the story occurs. The setting can be present, past, or future, as well as real or imaginary.

Characters

People or creatures with human characteristics are the characters in fiction. There are major characters, the ones that the story revolves around, and minor characters, those that play a role in the main characters' lives.

Theme

The theme is the message that the author is trying to get across to the reader. The theme is usually hidden within the story.

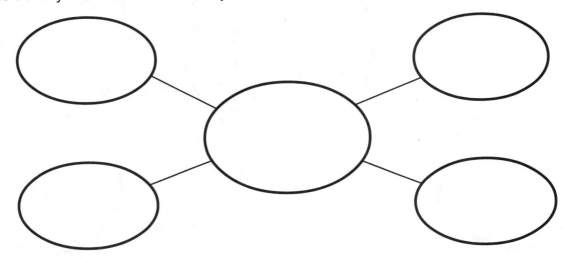

Name: _____ Date: _____

NOTE TAKING FROM TEXTBOOKS: WEB 2

Exercise: Read the following paragraph. When you are finished, fill in the web with your notes. Write the main idea in the center circle and the topic details in the other circles. Expand the web as needed.

Space Travel

Have you ever thought about traveling in outer space? In the future, travel to another planet may be as easy as travel to another country is now. If you travel to Mercury, you may want to take your suntan lotion with you. Mercury is the planet closest to the sun, and the temperature is 400 degrees Fahrenheit. Jupiter is the largest planet and could probably hold many tourists. If you traveled to Pluto, your vacation would last much longer because it takes 250 of our years for Pluto to travel around the sun once. Mars has two satellites that rotate around it; one satellite, Phobos, rises in the west and sets in the east. Mars is also called the red planet. Wherever you go, send us a postcard!

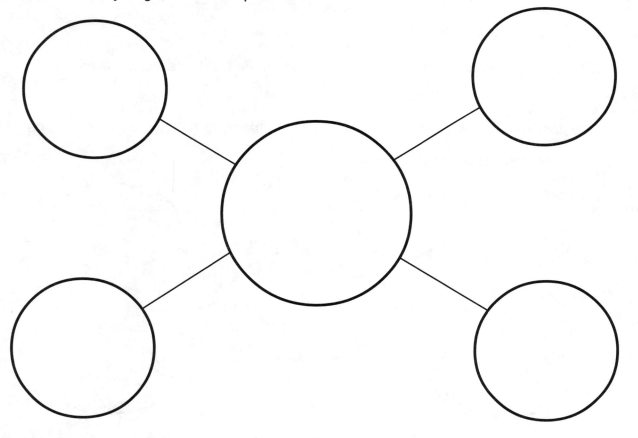

NOTE TAKING FROM NOVELS

When you sit down to read a novel or fictional writing for entertainment, you don't often think about taking notes. In your classroom, when you read a novel or fictional writing, it is usually for instruction, and you may need to take notes on the plot, on the characters, or possibly to compare this book to other books you have read. Often, you take notes to help in comprehension.

A novel or fictional writing doesn't have chapter headings, topic headings, words in boldface type, or captions under pictures. You need to use different strategies when taking notes.

Reading — As you read, you will look for information and write notes as soon as you come to something that is important. You can have your graphic organizer, chart, or web next to you and fill it in as you read or after you read a page or chapter.

Skimming — When you skim a page or chapter, you are looking for general information about a topic. For example, if you are working on characterization and need to get information about one of the characters, you can skim the chapter or section after you have read it. Your eyes are skimming over the text to find details about the character.

Scanning — As you read, you are looking for specific information. You can use scanning to go back in your reading to find vocabulary words you had difficulty with or names you need to know.

Name: _____ Date: _____

NOTE TAKING FROM NOVELS: VENN DIAGRAM 1

Exercise: Read the following story, and fill in the Venn diagram comparing and contrasting the two characters.

Carol has been my best friend since kindergarten. I remember the first day I met her. She was so cute in her pink shorts and T-shirt. Her blond hair was up in two pigtails. On the other hand, my brown hair hung straight, and I was always pushing it out of my eyes. I don't know why she was my best friend. The only thing we had in common were our dogs. They were from Mr. Mason's Labrador retriever. Carol always knew everyone at school. When we started junior high, it seemed she knew everyone from all the grade schools. She would pull me along and introduce me to people in the hall and at lunch. I'd blush and try to crawl back into my shell. Carol knew all the boys, and they flocked to her house. She said it was because they were friends with her brother. If that were true, I'd gladly trade my two sisters for a brother. I don't know how it happened—it must have been all the practicing I did with Carol—but I made cheerleader when she did. That's the thing about best friends, they can get you to do things you never would have tried on your own.

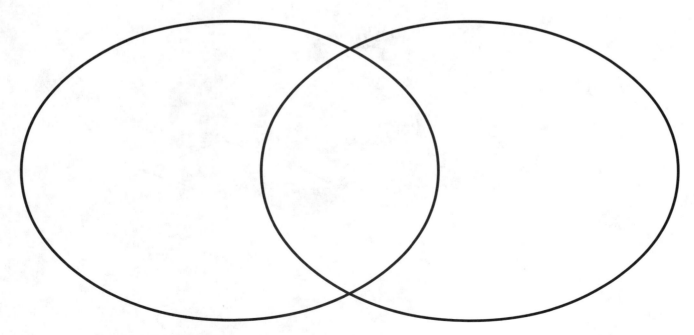

Name: _____ Date: _____

NOTE TAKING FROM NOVELS: VENN DIAGRAM 2

Exercise: Read the following story. Take notes using the Venn diagram to compare and contrast the two characters.

Alex and Nate were twins. They were very much alike, and at the same time, as different as night and day. Both of them played soccer, but Nate was a goalie and Alex played forward. Alex's favorite team was the Blazers, and Nate's favorite was the Gems. They even liked to study different things. Alex loved history, while Nate's favorite subject was art. Both of them got good grades in school. Of course, they looked a lot alike. They were the same height and had the same eye and hair color. Even though Nate didn't need glasses, Alex did. I don't know how that worked. Aren't twins supposed to be identical?

Name: _____ Date: _____

NOTE TAKING FROM NOVELS: SCAN 1

Exercise: Read each question. Then scan the following paragraph for the answer.

1. What is the Pizza House phone number? _____

     John Anderson worked at the Pizza House restaurant. He rode his bike to work every day. His job was to take the phone orders. He would answer the phone at 555-3939 and then ask for the order. The strangest request he ever received was for pineapple and anchovy pizza.

2. What is the price of the tapes? _____

     The discount music store was having a sale. They had a full-page ad in the Sunday newspaper. They were selling CDs for $6.99, tapes for $2.99, and cases from $3.00 to $9.99. Some of the boxed sets were 20% off. They were hoping for a huge crowd for the sale.

3. When was John Adams born? _____

     John Adams was the second president of the United States. His son John Quincy Adams was also president. John Adams was born in 1735 in the Massachusetts Bay Colony. He played a role in the writing of the Declaration of Independence.

Name: _____ Date: _____

NOTE TAKING FROM NOVELS: SCAN 2

Exercise: Read the following paragraphs. Then scan for the answers to the questions.

Dolley Madison was the wife of President James Madison. She had been married before to a man who died, leaving her with a son named Payne. Dolley had been brought up as a strict Quaker, but after her marriage to James Madison, she gave that up. She was known for giving wonderful parties at the White House and was an important part of the social scene. During the War of 1812, she escaped from the White House before the British burned it, taking a portrait of George Washington with her. To this day, the portrait that she saved hangs in the White House.

1. What religion had Dolley Madison been before her marriage to James? _____

Notre Dame has been a place I have always wanted to visit. When my French class planned a trip to Paris, I knew I had to go. I thought about the trip and my plan to visit Notre Dame. I had promised myself that that would be the first place I would visit when I got off the plane. Our guide had other plans, however, and we followed him around from one historic place to another. On our third day in Paris, I finally got my wish. Notre Dame was the most beautiful place I had ever seen. I quietly toured the inside and then took picture after picture of the outside. Then when the other students walked around the area, I just sat and stared until they came back for me.

2. When did the writer finally get to see Notre Dame? _____

Name: _____ Date: _____

NOTE TAKING FROM NOVELS: CHARACTER 1

Exercise: Read the following story. Fill in the chart at the end with your notes about the character. Add boxes as needed.

Grandfather

My grandfather was a smart man. He only went to school until the eighth grade, but he felt that education was the golden key to opportunity, so he tried to learn something new every day. He loved to do crossword puzzles and learned many new vocabulary words this way. He was always proud when one of his grandchildren asked about a word and he could tell them what it meant. Grandfather read the newspaper cover to cover every day. He felt you should know what was going on in the world and in your town. If he wondered where a city was that he read about, he looked it up in an atlas. He would play math games with us and see who could do multiplication the fastest. He always won, and he did the problems in his head! My grandfather only went to school through the eighth grade, but he was the smartest man I know.

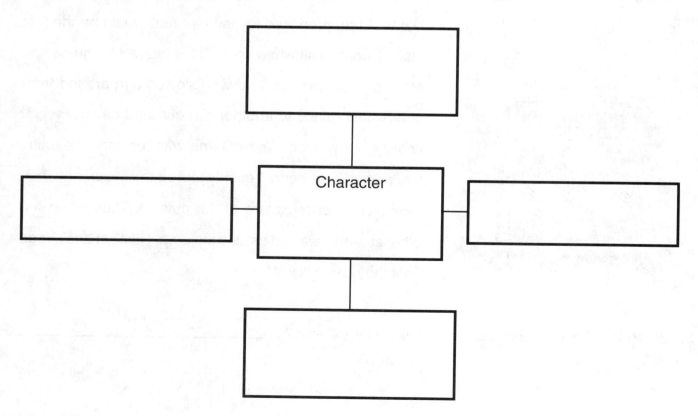

Character

Name: _____ Date: _____

NOTE TAKING FROM NOVELS: CHARACTER 2

Exercise: Read the following story. Fill in the chart at the end with your notes about the character. Add boxes as needed.

Esmerelda

Esmerelda was a beautiful Gypsy woman who always told fortunes at the local county fair. No one knew where she came from or why she moved here, and she never answered those questions when asked. She was always warm and sweet to anyone who visited her booth. She loved to read people's palms. No one who visited Esmerelda was ever expected to have a short life, and good fortune was always around the corner. Sometimes, though, my friends and I would see her in the diner downtown alone. She always stared out the window with a far-away look in her dark eyes, as if she were waiting for someone to appear out of the night.

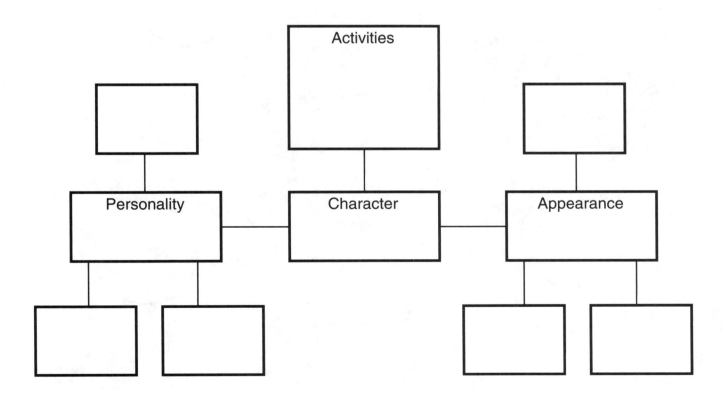

Name: _____ Date: _____

NOTE TAKING FROM NOVELS: WEB 1

Exercise: Read the following story. Take notes by filling in the web. Use or add circles as needed.

A tiger kitten was born at our local zoo recently. The newspaper wrote that the mother cat had finally moved around some so that people who came to the zoo could see the kitten. I finally convinced my friend Betsy that we should try to go see it. I love tigers, but she thinks that the primate house is the only place that's worth visiting. "But tiger kittens are so cute!" I told her. She thought that was true, but they aren't nearly as adorable as baby monkeys, and there are three little monkeys at the zoo, too. Besides, she told me, you can't get a good look at the tigers. Their pens are too large. The monkeys are right behind Plexiglas, and we can sit in the air conditioning. I suggested that we should be able to see them both.

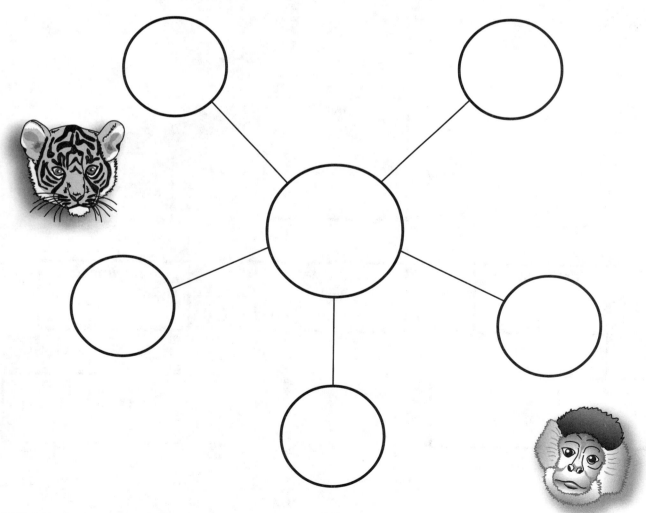

Name: _____   Date: _____

NOTE TAKING FROM NOVELS: WEB 2

Exercise: Read the following story. Take notes using the web. Use or add circles as needed.

My niece loves Easter egg hunts, but I keep telling her that they're nothing like the ones we had when I was a kid. Hers use plastic eggs that are full of candy, but mine always used hard-boiled eggs. My sister and I would dye them the night before and leave them on the kitchen counter in a basket. There was always at least one egg hidden in a drainpipe and another in a flowerpot somewhere by the door. When we were little, the eggs were hidden near the ground, but as we grew older, the eggs were up higher and hidden a little more completely. I don't know how the Easter Bunny would sneak into my house and hide those eggs, but he always managed, and he always manages for my niece as well.

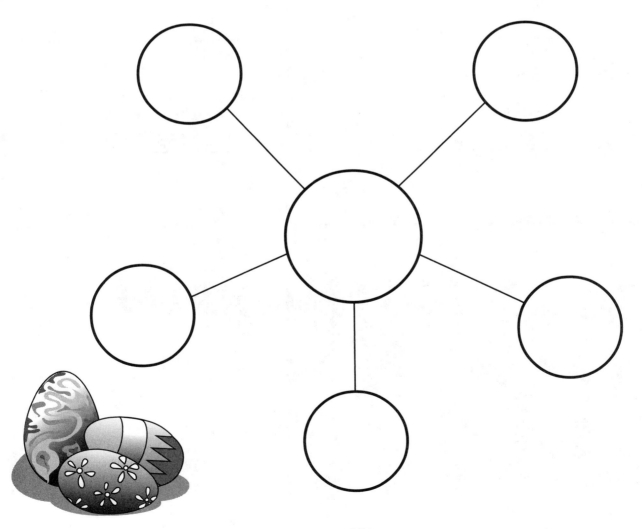

Name: _____ Date: _____

NOTE TAKING FROM NOVELS: SUMMARY

Exercise: Read the following story. Write a summary on the lines below.

I must have waited in line for four hours, but it was worth it. Season tickets to watch my school's football team were hard to come by, especially with all the other students and parents and visitors who wanted to watch the games. We have played well in other years, but we won the division championship last year, so tickets were even harder to get this year than last. The line moved at a snail's pace; luckily, it wasn't raining or cold. The people standing in the line with me were friendly, and we joked around and really got to know one another. I can hardly wait for the beginning of the season. I'll be in the stands, wearing my team's red and blue and cheering for all I'm worth.

_____

_____

_____

_____

_____

_____

NOTE TAKING FROM RESEARCH

Teachers often assign research papers to their students. A research paper is an informative report that uses a variety of resources: books, magazines, the Internet, newspapers, and videos to name a few. Being able to take good notes is vital to your success.

You should start the note-taking process as soon as you begin to read about your topic. Note taking is very important because you won't be able to remember all the information that you read.

Lined note cards are the easiest tools to use to help you keep your notes in order. Students often want to use a computer printout and highlight the important information instead of using note cards. This is not a good plan because various pieces of paper can be lost, but more importantly, there is information on a note card that will help you later to write the bibliography for your paper.

Follow these guidelines when taking notes while researching.

1. Read the selection that you will be taking notes on.

2. In the upper left-hand corner of your card, write the topic of the card. For example, "history," or "crops," or "early years."

3. In the upper right-hand corner, write the number that corresponds to the bibliography card. For example, if this is the third book you have gotten information from, your bibliography card would be number three, so you put a "3" in the upper right-hand corner. This helps so you don't have to write all the bibliography information each time.

4. Write note card information in your own words. If you use a direct quote, make sure it is in quotation marks.

5. Write the page number at the bottom of the card.

6. Bibliography cards are used to keep track of information needed to write a bibliography. You need very specific notes to write the bibliography card. The information needed for a bibliography card is usually found in the front of the newspaper, magazine, or book. Generally, a bibliography card has the resource number in the upper right-hand corner. It also includes the author, last name first; the title of the resource; the publisher; the place it was published; and the date it was published. There are many books that will help you know what to write and the order in which to write a bibliography card.

Name: _____ Date: _____

NOTE TAKING FROM RESEARCH: NOTE CARDS 1

Exercise: Read the following paragraph. Decide what information should go on each note card.

     In the fall of the year, the most popular sport in the United States is football. The game is played on a rectangular field 100 yards long and 160 feet wide. Football is played with two teams, each with 11 players. The football is made of leather and is long with pointed ends. The object of the game is to move the ball down the field by passing the football or running with the ball. The game is divided into four quarters, each 15 minutes long. The game takes longer than an hour, however, because the clock is stopped at various times for a score, a ball out of bounds, or for a penalty. In football, you can get points for a touchdown, which is six points, a field goal, which is worth three points, a one-point kick after a touchdown, or a two-point conversion after a touchdown. There are many different plays and strategies in a football game. This makes for an interesting and exciting game.

Game length

Points

Field

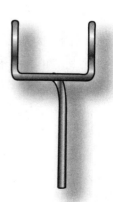

Name: _____ Date: _____

NOTE TAKING FROM RESEARCH: NOTE CARDS 2

Exercise: Read the following information, and then fill in the note cards. The topic has been done for you.

Spain

Agriculture

Farming in Spain can be difficult because of the terrain. Spain produces many crops. The two main crops are wheat and barley. Some other crops are grapes, potatoes, and oranges. Some people raise livestock, including goats and sheep.

Crops

Tourism

Many people visit Spain. This is especially true since the Olympics were held in Barcelona in 1992. Spain offers many opportunities for visitors. There are mountains and coastlines where people vacation.

Olympics

Name: _____ Date: _____

Note Taking From Research: Bibliography Cards

Exercise: Use the following information to fill in the bibliography cards.

1. The first book you use for research: Jeff Brown wrote it in 1992. The title of the book is <u>Journey to Mars</u>, and Elementary Press published it in Dallas, Texas.

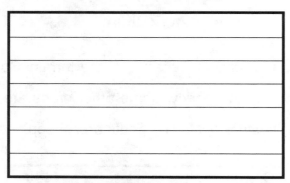

2. The fourth resource is a magazine article called "Space Exploration." You found it in the May 2001 issue of <u>Science Adventures</u>. It was written by Steven Capp and was on pages 38–40.

3. Your eighth resource is a newspaper article from <u>The Sterling Sentinel</u> called "Farmer Sees UFO." The article didn't have an author, but it was from the October 28, 1999 issue, section A, page 2.

34

NOTE TAKING FROM ONLINE SOURCES

Taking notes from a computer source is much the same as taking notes from your text. You need to read the title, headings, captions, charts, vocabulary words, and dates, just as you would with a textbook.

When you take notes from online sources, there are other things you need to look for, too.

1. Read who the author of the source is. What are his or her credentials? Does he or she have an address where he or she can be contacted? Do you know who sponsored the site, and do they show bias?

2. When was the site last updated? You can usually find this date at the bottom of the page, or there may be a copyright date. These will help you know how old the information is. In some reports, like one on Abraham Lincoln, it may not make a difference how old the information is. However, if your report is about something that changes often, like science or technology, it will make a difference.

3. Look for accuracy in the online source. It is a good idea to check statements in a couple of other sources to make sure the information is accurate.

To organize your online notes, you can print out the whole website or a section of the website, and then highlight the information you need. This can be difficult because you will have many papers and probably extra information, but you should have all the information needed for the bibliography on those papers. You can take notes on note cards or in your binder directly from the computer. Make sure you include all the information needed for the bibliography. A third way is to copy and paste the necessary information into a word processing document. Doing it like this, you also need to make sure you copy and paste all the information you need for the bibliography. You teacher will tell you which way is preferred.

Name: _____   Date: _____

Note Taking From Online Sources: Practice 1

Exercise: Read the following section of a web page. Take notes by filling in the requested information below.

http://www.mousehouse.org

THE MOUSE OF THE HOUSE

By Jim White

Eeek! Do you ever hear that sound in your house? Well, that's probably because someone saw a mouse in your house.

Description

The small gray or brown mouse that comes into a house is called a house mouse. They are about six to seven inches long and weigh a few ounces.

Habitat

During the spring and summer, a house mouse is usually outdoors and lives off the land, eating seeds. When fall comes, they find ways to get into your house or garage where it is warmer. They live off grains and food in your pantry and crumbs off the floor.

Contact: jwhite12@net.org   last updated: 03.06.03

1. The title of the website _____

2. The headings _____

3. Important detail _____

4. Important detail _____

5. Important detail _____

6. Vocabulary words _____

7. Author _____

8. Last updated _____

9. URL _____

10. Contact address _____

Name: _____ Date: _____

NOTE TAKING FROM ONLINE SOURCES: PRACTICE 2

Exercise: Read the following section of a web page. Take notes by filling in the requested information below.

<u>http://www.gwash.org</u>

THE FIRST PRESIDENT

Childhood

George Washington was born in Virginia on February 22, 1732. He was tall and strong. He liked mathematics and music. George was taught to be a surveyor by his half-brother. His father died in 1743 when George was eleven.

President Washington

George Washington was elected President of the United States in 1789. It was a unanimous decision. His vice president was John Adams. He was elected to a second term in 1793 but did not run for a third term.

Written by Ann Current   contact: acurrent@lulee.net   copyright © 1999

1. The title of the website _____

2. The headings _____

3. Important detail _____

4. Important detail _____

5. Important detail _____

6. Vocabulary words _____

7. Author _____

8. Last updated _____

9. URL _____

10. Contact address _____

37

NOTE TAKING IN CLASS

When you are listening to your teacher, it is important to take notes about what he or she is saying. Listening is not enough. You need notes to help you remember later what was said. You need to write clearly so that you know what you wrote when you later look back at the notes.

Things to remember when taking notes in class:

1. Make sure that you are prepared to take notes. Have a section in your binder for the class and class notes, or have a separate spiral notebook just for that class. Being organized will help you find the notes when you need them.

2. Write down the date and the topic at the beginning of the page. Starting with a clean piece of paper will also help you keep your notes organized for the topic.

3. It there are notes on the board, write them down with space after them so that you can add what the teacher says about them.

4. Don't try to write down everything the teacher says. Listen for clue words, such as "this is key" or "this is important" or "the main idea is." Listen for dates and definitions, and also listen for people's names and what they did or why they are important. Also, listen for specific terms.

5. If there are steps talked about, write the steps and the words or phrases to help you remember what happened at each step. Teachers will often say, "the steps are …"

6. Sit near the front of the class or room so that you are able to hear the teacher, see the board, and stay focused.

TEACHER IDEAS FOR NOTE-TAKING ACTIVITIES

To help students taking notes in class, try these ideas. You can have students take notes in several ways: taking lecture notes, summarizing, finding the main idea and supporting points, using chronological order, or making a web.

1. Read a magazine article to the students, and have them take notes as you read.

2. Watch a travel video on a particular country, and have the students take notes as they watch.

3. Videotape a cooking show, and have students take notes of the ingredients and order of preparation and anything else that they think is important.

4. Read a newspaper article to the students, and have them take notes.

5. Watch a videotape of the news. Have the students take notes as an outline.

6. Read an editorial to the students. Have them draw a web of the main point and the supporting details.

7. Read an encyclopedia article about a person. Have the students take notes and then put them in chronological order.

RESOURCE/REFERENCE

Summary: A shortened version of what you have read. It contains the main idea written in your own words. It may also include some details, but these should also be written in your own words. A summary is usually three or four sentences long.

Outline: A listing of main ideas, subtopics, important facts, and information that is written under headings and subheadings. Usually Roman numerals are used for the topic, capital letters are used for the main ideas, the subtopics are written with Arabic numerals, and lowercase letters are used for the details in outlines.

> *Example:* I. Chapter Title
>   A. Main Idea
>   1. Subtopic
>   a. detail
>   b. detail
>   2. Subtopic
>   a. detail
>   b. detail

Web: An organizational tool for taking notes that has the main idea in a circle or square with the subtopics in smaller circles or squares and the details in even smaller circles or squares. They are connected to each other with lines, and they look a little like a spider web.

Example:

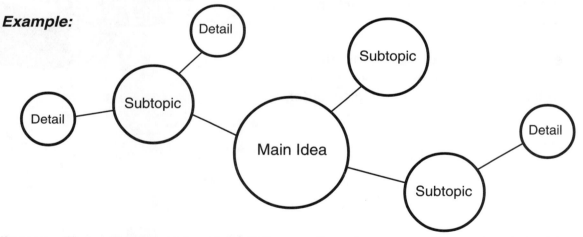

Venn diagram: Two or three overlapping circles or other shapes used to compare and contrast ideas. Where the shapes overlap, things that compare (are alike) are written, and in the outer parts of the shapes, things that contrast (are different) are written.

Example:

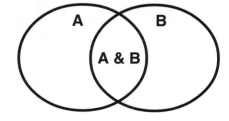

RESOURCE/REFERENCE (CONT.)

Table: Used to organize notes that have a main idea and/or main character and many supporting details. The main idea is written as the table, and the details are the legs that support the table. This can also be used to compare two ideas by drawing two tables.

Example:

Main Idea				
Detail	Detail	Detail	Detail	Detail

Lists: Used in note taking for a process of steps. This can be used in science or math where there are steps to a solution of a problem or an experiment. Lists would also be used for the steps to a climax or resolution in a novel. The lists are usually in 1, 2, 3, or A, B, C, order.

Example:

1. First step   or   A. First step
2. Second step   B. Second step
3. Third step   C. Third step

Chronological Order: Arranging notes in the order in which they happened. This is most often used in history or other subjects where the events are dated. Chronological order is a time line, starting from the oldest date to the most recent. Sometimes the dates are only days or even hours apart. Other times, they are years or decades apart. You can either do it by dates or by first, second, third, and so on.

Example: 1776 – American Revolution

1812 – War of 1812

1861 – Civil War

Cause and Effect: Arranging notes in an order that details the causes and then the effects. For example, because this happened, this resulted.

Example:

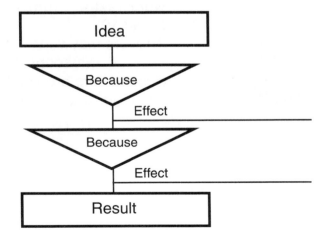

ANSWER KEYS

Note Taking From Textbooks: Practice 1 (page 4)
Some answers may vary.
Topic: Abraham Lincoln
Heading: Early Life
Important dates: 1809 born, 1816 mother died, 1830 moved to Illinois
Important names: Thomas and Nancy Lincoln, Sarah
Vocabulary words: rail-splitter
Important fact: Born in Kentucky
Important fact: Not much formal education
Important fact: Loved to read
Important fact: Had an older sister

Note Taking From Textbooks: Practice 2 (page 5)
Some answers may vary.
Topic: Fuel
Heading: Solid Fuels
Vocabulary words: anthracite, lignite, bituminous
Types of solid fuel: coal, wood, charcoal, peat
Important detail: wood—little heat
Important detail: three types of coal
Important detail: Charcoal—from wood
Important detail: Peat—smoky; from vegetation

Note Taking From Textbooks: Practice 3 (page 6)
Some answers may vary.
Topic: Alaska
Dates: Purchased 1867; Gold discovered 1880
Vocabulary words: petroleum, Gold Rush
Important detail: Seward's Folly, Seward's Icebox
Important detail: Gold discovered 1880
Important detail: Largest state
Important detail: National parks
Important detail: Oil industry

Note Taking From Textbooks: Practice 4 (page 7)
Some answers may vary.
Topic: Aluminum
Heading: Uses
Vocabulary words: metallic, alloy, conducts
Important detail: Used in construction
Important detail: 7% of Earth's crust
Important detail: Conducts heat/electricity
Important detail: lightweight
Important detail: Used in space travel

Note Taking From Textbooks: Chronological Order 1 (page 8)
April 12, 1861: Fort Sumter
July 21, 1861: Manassas (Battle of Bull Run)
March 8, 1862: *Merrimack* and *Monitor*
July 1, 1863–July 3, 1863: Gettysburg
April 9, 1865: Surrender

Note Taking From Textbooks: Chronological Order 2 (page 9)
November 19, 1831: Born
1858: Marriage
December 1863–December 1879: Congressman
January 1880: Elected senator
March 4, 1881: Became president
July 2, 1881: Shot by assassin
September 19, 1881: Died

Note Taking From Textbooks: Summary 1 (page 10)
Answers may vary.

A telescope makes objects appear closer. There are two types, refracting, which bends light, and reflecting, which reflects light.

Note Taking From Textbooks: Summary 2 (page 11)

Answers may vary.

Runoff is when more rain falls than can be absorbed by the land. This is because the ground is saturated or paved. All this water eventually goes back to the ocean.

Note Taking From Textbooks: Outline 1 (page 12)

1. I
2. IV
3. I
4. II
5. III
6. I
7. IV
8. II
9. IV
10. III

Note Taking From Textbooks: Outline 2 (page 13)

1. I
2. III
3. III
4. II
5. I
6. II
7. III
8. I
9. III
10. II

Note Taking From Textbooks: Table (page 14) Answers may vary.

Garter snakes				
yellow stripes	18–30 inches long	thick bodies	eat frogs, tadpoles, & small mammals	don't lay eggs

Note Taking From Textbooks: Cause and Effect (page 15)

Answers may vary.

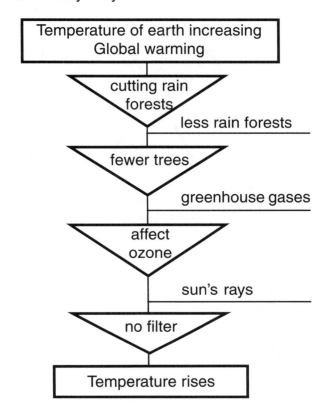

Note Taking From Textbooks: Venn Diagram 1 (page 16)

Answers may vary.

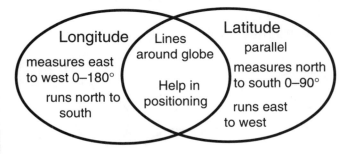

Note Taking From Textbooks: Venn Diagram 2 (page 17)
Answers may vary.

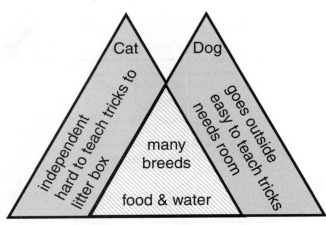

Note Taking From Textbooks: List (page 18)
Answers may vary.
1. Get out ingredients.
2. Get out utensils.
3. Mix butter and sugar.
4. Add eggs and vanilla, stir.
5. Add flour, baking soda, salt; mix.
6. Stir in chocolate chips.
7. Drop by spoonfuls on cookie sheet.
8. Bake.
9. Cool.
10. Eat.

Note Taking From Textbooks: Web 1 (page 19)
Answers may vary.

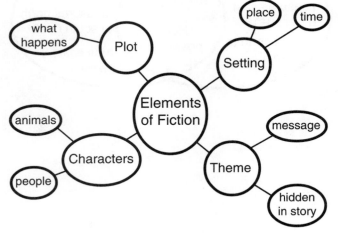

Note Taking From Textbooks: Web 2 (page 20)
Answers may vary.

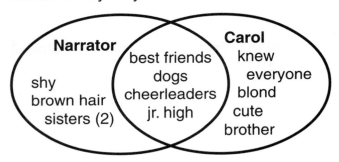

Note Taking From Novels: Venn Diagram 1 (page 22)
Answers may vary.

Narrator
shy
brown hair
sisters (2)

best friends
dogs
cheerleaders
jr. high

Carol
knew
everyone
blond
cute
brother

Note Taking From Novels: Venn Diagram 2 (page 23)
Answers may vary.

Alex
team:
 Blazers
forward
history
glasses

soccer
good grades
same height,
eye, & hair
color

Nate
team:
 Gems
goalie
art

Note Taking From Novels: Scan 1 (page 24)
1. 555-3939
2. $2.99
3. 1735

Note Taking From Novels: Scan 1 (page 25)
1. Quaker
2. On the third day in Paris

Note Taking From Novels: Character 1 (page 26)
Answers may vary.

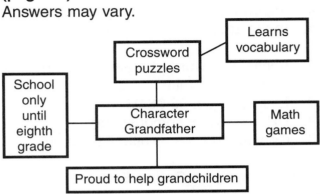

Note Taking From Novels: Character 2 (page 27)
Answers may vary.

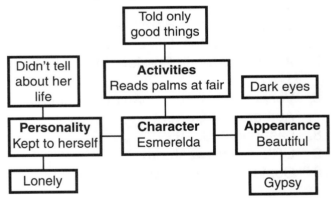

Note Taking From Novels: Web 1 (page 28)
Answers may vary.

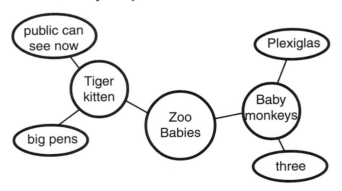

Note Taking From Novels: Web 2 (page 29)
Answers may vary.

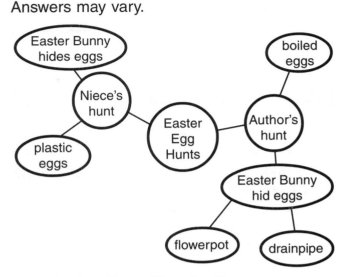

Note Taking From Novels: Summary (page 30)
Answers may vary.

Season tickets were hard to get because the team had won the division championship the year before, but the author got them after waiting in line four hours.

Note Taking From Research: Note Cards 1 (page 32)

Game length:
Four quarters – 15 minutes long
Game takes longer than 1 hour
because the clock is stopped

Points:
Touchdown – 6 points
Field goal – 3 points
Kick after – 1 point
Conversion – 2 points

Field:
Rectangle – 100 yards by 160 feet

Note Taking From Research: Note Cards 2 (page 33)

Crops:
  Main – wheat, barley
  Others – grapes, potatoes, oranges

Olympics:
  Held in Barcelona in 1992

Note Taking From Research: Bibliography Cards (page 34)

1.

(1)

Brown, Jeff. Journey to Mars.
  Dallas: Elementary Press, 1992.

2.

(4)

Capp, Steven. "Space Exploration."
  Science Adventures.
  May 2001: 38–40.

3.

(8)

"Farmer Sees UFO." The Sterling
  Sentinel. 28 Oct. 1999, sec. A: 2.

Note Taking From Online Sources: Practice 1 (page 36)

Detail answers may vary.
1. Title: The Mouse of the House
2. Headings: Description, Habitat
3. Important detail: gray or brown
4. Important detail: weighs a few ounces
5. Important detail: comes inside in fall and winter
6. Vocabulary words: house mouse, habitat
7. Author: Jim White
8. Last updated: 03.06.03
9. URL: www.housemouse.org
10. Contact address: jwhite12@net.org

Note Taking From Online Sources: Practice 2 (page 37)

Detail answers may vary.
1. Title: The First President
2. Headings: Childhood, President Washington
3. Important detail: Born Feb. 22, 1732
4. Important detail: Liked math and music
5. Important detail: President from 1789 to 1797
6. Vocabulary words: unanimous, surveyor
7. Author: Ann Current
8. Last updated: 1999
9. URL: www.gwash.org
10. Contact address: acurrent@lulee.net